D0229584

A PARRAGON BOOK
Published by Parragon Books, Unit 13-17 Avonbridge Trading Estate,
Atlantic Road, Avonmouth, Bristol BS11 9QD
Produced by The Templar Company plc, Pippbrook Mill,
London Road, Dorking, Surrey RH4 1JE
Copyright © 1994 Parragon Book Service Limited
All rights reserved
Designed by Janie Louise Hunt
Edited by Caroline Steeden
Printed and bound in Italy
ISBN 1-85813-678-4

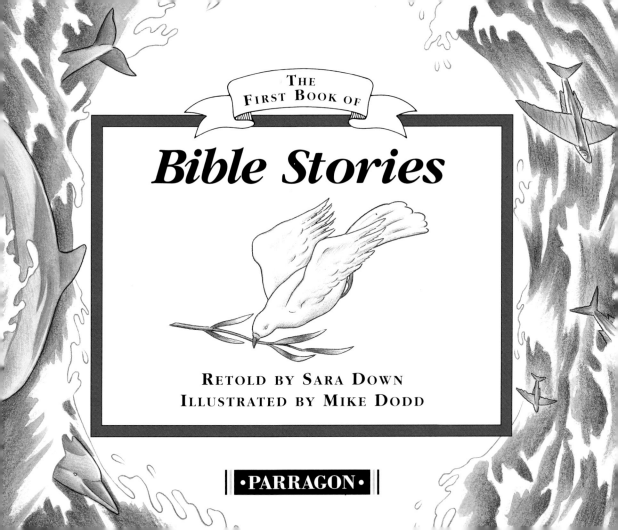

The
FIRST BOOK OF

Bible Stories

RETOLD BY SARA DOWN
ILLUSTRATED BY MIKE DODD

•PARRAGON•

*This Book
Belongs to*

_____

_____

CONTENTS

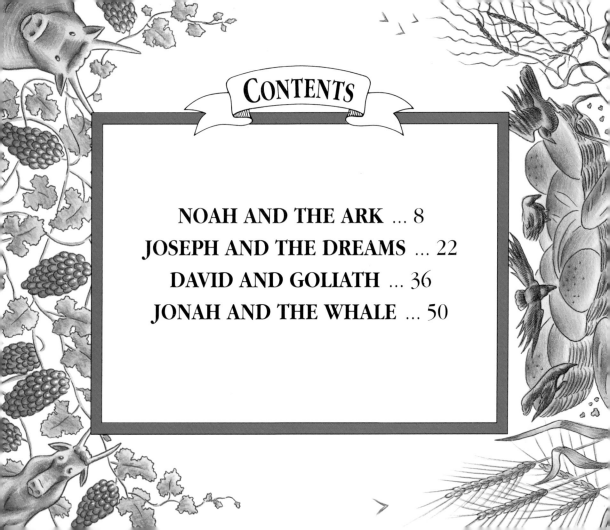

NOAH AND THE ARK

God looked over the world he had created, and saw that his people had become selfish, thinking only of themselves, and little about him. They often became angry and fought with each other.

At this time there lived a man called Noah. He was a gentle, kind man who tried hard to live a good life. God was pleased with Noah and looked on him with love. God said to Noah, "I'm very sad to see that my people have become wicked. I must get rid of the evil in the world, and the only way to do it is to destroy all living things."

9

However, God did not want to lose Noah, so he told him to build a huge boat, called an ark. "Build it with the wood of the Cypress tree," God said. "Cover it with reeds and coat it with tar. Make it four hundred and fifty feet long, seventy-five feet wide, and forty-five feet high. It needs a roof and a door in its side, and it must have three decks." Noah respected God and did not question his commands. God told him, "I will send a great flood. It will cover everything as far as the eye can see and destroy all life on earth. But I will make a special promise to you, Noah, we will call it our covenant.

"Enter the ark with your wife, your sons and your sons' wives, and take with you two of every kind of living creature, all those that crawl on the earth, each kind of insect and reptile, each beast and bird. And gather every type of edible food to keep you and the animals alive."

Noah did as God had commanded him. He and his three sons, Shem, Ham and Japheth and their wives, built the ark. They cut wood from the mighty Cypress tree and built three levels, with a door and window just as God had described. Next they gathered the food. All types of fruit, including melons, bananas, and grapes, unlevened bread, hay and oats, grain and leaves were brought into the ark and carefully stored in preparation for the big flood. At last all was ready.

Then God said to Noah, "In seven days I will send rain to fall on the earth for forty days and forty nights, and the

water will rise up and cover everything." Noah and his
family entered the ark as they had been told to. God
called all the creatures to come to Noah, and they also
entered the ark. Each pair of animals went in two by

two; great elephants with their trunks swinging as they
lumbered along, small monkeys chattering with
excitement, camels and horses, cows and sheep, llamas
and antelopes, and beautiful birds with brightly coloured
feathers. The animals walked, slithered, jumped and
crawled their way onto the ark to live with Noah and be
saved from the flood.

The rain fell from the sky, and all the springs of the earth opened. The water rose up and became very deep. It covered all the land, until even the mountain tops disappeared. The rain fell for forty days and forty nights, just as God had said it would, and the flood destroyed all living things upon the earth, except for Noah, his family and the animals in the ark. The ark was tossed about on the dark water, the waves bounced and crashed against it. The wind howled and the earth was dark and full of sadness.

But God did not forget Noah and all the animals. He sent a strong wind to blow over the earth and quieten the storm. The rain stopped falling and the springs dried up. The water slowly retreated until finally the ark touched the top of a mountain in Ararat. The water level went down slowly, and soon other mountain tops could been seen.

Noah decided it was time to see if the land was dry enough for him and his family to leave the ark, so he opened his window and released a raven. If there was any dry land the raven would not return. However, there was no dry land, and the raven could only fly around above the water. Eventually it grew too tired to fly and returned to the ark.

Noah waited for another seven days and then released a dove, but like the raven, the dove could find no place to land, and so it returned to the ark. For another seven days Noah waited, then released the dove again. This time the dove returned with a freshly picked olive leaf.

Noah knew for certain then that there was dry land, and that the waters had dried up, because olive trees only grow in valleys. Just to be certain he waited another seven days, and released the dove once more. This time the dove did not return and Noah knew that it was now time to leave. Noah opened the door of the ark and looked out. The land was dry.

God said to Noah, "All of you can come out of the ark now and start a new life on the earth. The animals will multiply and fill the earth."

Slowly the animals came out of the ark.
They were pleased to be on land again.
Everything looked fresh and new.
It was like spring, the flowers
had blossomed and the trees
were beginning to grow fruit,
the land was green and warm.

Noah built an altar and made an offering to God to thank him for saving his family and the animals and for providing such a beautiful new land for them to live in.

When God smelt the sweet odour of the offerings that Noah had prepared, he thought to himself, "Never again will I destroy the earth and all its living creatures. From this day on seed time and harvest, summer and winter, day and night shall never end."

God made this promise to mankind, and to show that his promise would last forever he put a rainbow high in the sky and said, "This shall be the sign of the promise I have made to all people. Whenever there is both sun and rain in the sky, the rainbow will appear as a symbol of our everlasting covenant."

Noah lived a long time after the flood. The animals spread over the earth, just as God had said. Noah's sons, Hem, Sham and Japheth had sons of their own and they became fathers of the nations of the earth. A whole new world had begun.

JOSEPH AND THE DREAMS

Joseph lived in Canaan with his father, Jacob. He was Jacob's favourite son, and his brothers hated him because of this. Jacob showed his love for Joseph by making him a long, flowing cloak of many bright colours, which made Joseph's brothers even more jealous. They were cruel to him, and never let him join in with them.

Joseph had many dreams, which he told his brothers about. This made them even angrier, as Joseph's dreams seemed to say that he was more important than them. They thought Joseph was very big-headed.

Joseph's brothers went to look after their father's sheep leaving Joseph behind. But Jacob was worried about them and said to Joseph, "Go and find your brothers, see if they are well and bring me back the news." Joseph set off to find them, but before he reached them, they caught sight of him in the distance and began to plot against him. "Here comes that dreamer," they said, "now's our chance to kill him. Let's throw him into a pit and say a wild beast has eaten him. Then we'll see how important his dreams are!" When Joseph arrived they stripped him of his beautiful long cloak and threw him into an empty pit, with no food or water.

Just then the brothers saw an Ishmaelite caravan coming. Judah said to the others, "We will gain nothing by killing Joseph and hiding his death. Let's sell him to the Ishmaelites. After all, we shouldn't harm him, for he is our brother." The others agreed, so they sold Joseph to the Ishmaelites, who took him to Egypt with them.

Joseph's brothers took his brightly-coloured cloak, tore it and dipped it in goat's blood. Then they took it to their father and said, "Do you recognise this?" Jacob did recognise it, and replied,"It is Joseph's cloak. A wild beast has killed and eaten him." Jacob was full of sadness. "I will go to my grave mourning the death of my son," he said, and he wept bitterly.

Meanwhile, Joseph had been sold in Egypt to Potiphar, the captain of Pharaoh's guard. Pharaoh was the ruler of Egypt. Potiphar saw that Joseph was blessed by the Lord, and that everything he did was successful, so he put him in charge of his house. Joseph was a handsome young man, and Potiphar's wife took a liking to him, but Joseph was honourable, and would not deceive his master. Potiphar's wife lied about Joseph, and said he had approached her. Potiphar was very angry with Joseph, and had him thrown into Pharoah's prison, without listening to his protests.

It so happened that Pharoah's butler and baker had been jailed for offending Pharoah. One night both of the men had dreams which greatly disturbed them, but neither they nor anyone else knew what the dreams meant. They asked everyone in the prison, but no one could help. "Tell them to me," said Joseph, "I can help you." The butler said, "I dreamt there was a grape vine in front of me, and as I watched three branches of the vine blossomed into ripe grapes. I picked these grapes, crushed them and poured the juice into Pharaoh's cup." Joseph knew what this dream meant. He said, "The three branches that you saw represent three days. After that time Pharaoh will take you back as his butler, and you will serve him with wine just as you did before you were put into prison. Now that I have told you this, remember me when you are with Pharoah. Tell him about me and help me to get out of here."

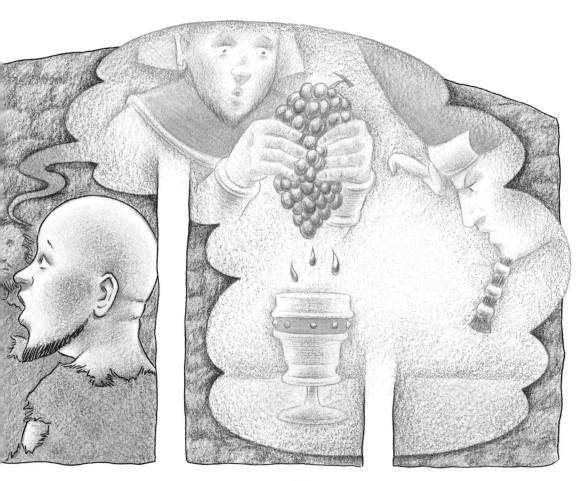

Then the baker said, "In my dream I had three baskets of bread on my head. They were full with all different kinds of bread but as I walked along the birds were pecking at the bread and eating it." Joseph looked sadly at the baker. "It means that in three days Pharaoh will order that you are taken and killed, and the birds will peck at you," he said.

Three days had passed since Joseph interpreted the dreams. It was Pharaoh's birthday and a huge feast was being held. Pharaoh took the butler from the prison and gave him back his job, but Pharaoh had his guards take the poor baker and kill him, just as Joseph had said. The butler was so pleased to be out of prison that he forgot all about Joseph, and did not mention him to Pharaoh.

Almost two years had passed, when Pharaoh had a disturbing dream. He was standing by the river Nile,

when seven fat cows came up from the river, and began to graze on the grassy bank. But soon afterwards seven thin cows came out of the river and ate the fat cows. Pharaoh woke up, but soon fell asleep again and had a second dream.

This time he saw seven ears of corn, which were ripe and full, but growing up under them, were seven ears of shrivelled, thin corn, which swallowed up the ripe corn. When Pharaoh woke in the morning he was deeply alarmed by his dreams. He called together his wise men to tell him what his dreams meant, but none of them knew. Suddenly the butler remembered Joseph, and said to Pharoah, "When I was in prison with the chief baker, we both had dreams which no one understood except a young slave, and his explanations came true."

Pharaoh immediately sent for Joseph to be brought from the dungeons. He said, "I have had two dreams and no one knows what they mean. I have been told that you can interpret them." Joseph replied, "I cannot interpret them myself, but God will tell me what they mean, so that I can tell you." Pharaoh told Joseph all that he had dreamt and Joseph listened carefully. Then he said, "Although you had two dreams, they have one meaning. The seven good cows, and the seven ripe ears of corn, mean that your lands will have seven years of good harvest, the earth will produce a lot of food, and everyone will have plenty to eat. But the seven thin cows, and seven shrivelled ears of corn, mean that after the good years there will be seven years of famine, with no crops, and the people will starve. God has sent you these dreams so you can rule your country wisely. You need someone to take charge of the harvest, collecting food each year of the good harvest and storing it safely, so that during the years of famine it can be given to the people."

Pharaoh was pleased with Joseph and chose him to look after the food supplies, saying, "Take charge of my household. All my servants will do as you tell them, and only I will have greater authority than you. Collect the harvest, and keep it safe until it is needed. The lives of my people will depend on you and you shall be highly rewarded for taking care of them."

Pharaoh dressed Joseph in fine clothes, and hung a long, gold chain around his neck. Joseph took the abundant food during the good years of harvest, and stored it. Huge mountains of food were collected. When the seven years of poor harvest came, it affected all the lands of the world, and only in Egypt was there enough food for the people to eat. Joseph was a careful and wise man, and he gave everyone a measure of grain, so that no one in his land starved. Pharaoh saw that he had made a good choice, and that Joseph's God was a true and mighty God.

DAVID AND GOLIATH

A long time ago, in the land of Israel, there was a great disturbance. The Philistines, who were a group of people living in a neighbouring land, wanted to rule Israel themselves. So they gathered a huge army and travelled into Israel intending to occupy it. King Saul, the ruler of Israel, knew of the Philistines' plans and gathered his own army to protect his land.

There was to be a huge war. Each army prepared for the fight, cleaning their swords and shields ready for the battle. On the day it was due to begin the armies lined up

on opposite sides of the valley facing each other, waiting for the command to send them into battle. The Philistines were feeling confident because they had a champion fighter to challenge the Israelites. His name was Goliath and he was over nine feet tall. On his head, he wore a bronze helmet. He had bronze armour to protect his body, and he carried a bronze dagger and a bronze spear, heavier and larger than any of the Israelites' weapons. He looked mean, nasty, and worst of all, unbeatable.

Goliath stood in front of the Israelites and shouted, "I am a mighty warrior. I demand that you choose a man to fight me. If he kills me in a fair fight, then all Philistines will become your slaves; but if I kill him, then you Israelites shall be our slaves."

The Israelites were afraid of this huge man and terrified by what he said. Not a single Israelite warrior wanted to fight him. Every day for forty days, Goliath came forward from the Philistine camp and shouted his challenge to the Israelites, but still nobody wanted to fight him.

At that time there lived an old man called Jesse who had eight sons. The three eldest were called Eliab, Abindab and Shammah, and the youngest was David. The three eldest sons went to Judah to support King Saul's Israelite army and join the fighting, while David stayed at home in Bethlehem to tend the sheep.

Jesse was concerned about his sons away at battle, so one day he sent David to find his brothers and bring back news of them. David set off early the next morning after asking a friend to guard the sheep while he was away. He travelled for several days along the dusty road, until he

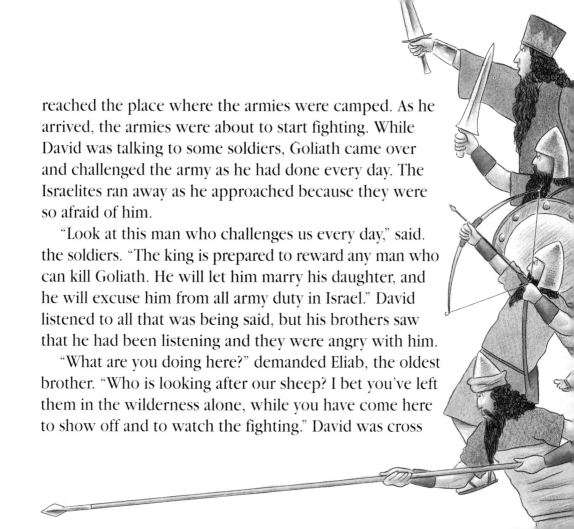

reached the place where the armies were camped. As he
arrived, the armies were about to start fighting. While
David was talking to some soldiers, Goliath came over
and challenged the army as he had done every day. The
Israelites ran away as he approached because they were
so afraid of him.

"Look at this man who challenges us every day," said.
the soldiers. "The king is prepared to reward any man who
can kill Goliath. He will let him marry his daughter, and
he will excuse him from all army duty in Israel." David
listened to all that was being said, but his brothers saw
that he had been listening and they were angry with him.

"What are you doing here?" demanded Eliab, the oldest
brother. "Who is looking after our sheep? I bet you've left
them in the wilderness alone, while you have come here
to show off and to watch the fighting." David was cross

with his brother for speaking so harshly to him. He replied, "I am only asking about the giant Philistine, am I not allowed to do even that?"

David was overheard talking about Goliath. It was reported to King Saul, who called David to him. David felt anxious at meeting such a great man as the King, but he said, "You must not give up, I will fight this Philistine."

Saul replied, "You are only a boy, you cannot fight this man who has been fighting all his life." But David knew God was on his side and he felt confident. He said, "Sir, I am a shepherd. When a lion or bear takes one of my father's sheep, I go after it, attack it and rescue the sheep. If the creature turns on me, then I seize it and fight with it until it is dead. This Philistine does not frighten me, and as he has insulted the army of God, I will fight him. The Lord has saved me from the bear and the lion, he will also save me from this man."

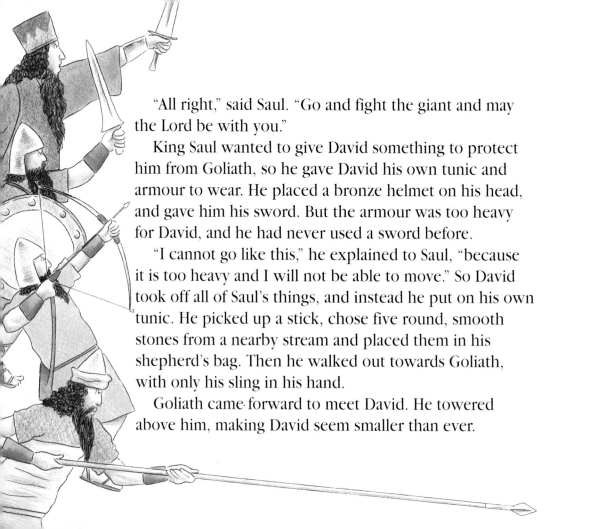

"All right," said Saul. "Go and fight the giant and may the Lord be with you."

King Saul wanted to give David something to protect him from Goliath, so he gave David his own tunic and armour to wear. He placed a bronze helmet on his head, and gave him his sword. But the armour was too heavy for David, and he had never used a sword before.

"I cannot go like this," he explained to Saul, "because it is too heavy and I will not be able to move." So David took off all of Saul's things, and instead he put on his own tunic. He picked up a stick, chose five round, smooth stones from a nearby stream and placed them in his shepherd's bag. Then he walked out towards Goliath, with only his sling in his hand.

Goliath came forward to meet David. He towered above him, making David seem smaller than ever.

He looked David up and down, and asked if it was joke sending such a small boy to fight a champion.

"Do you think that I am a fool? You have come to fight me with sticks and stones, but I have my sword and armour, and I will easily kill you. And when I have, I shall leave your body in the wilderness to be eaten by the birds and beasts."

David answered, "I am not afraid of you, even though you are a mighty champion. You have little to protect you compared to me for I have come with the power of the Lord, the God of the army which you have threatened. It is with His power that I shall kill you, and it is you who shall be left for the animals to eat. Then all the world will know that there is a God in Israel. This is not a war that can be won by spears and swords. Only the power of God will decide who is to win."

Goliath had heard enough and began to move towards David, who quickly put his hand into his bag. Taking out a stone he put it into his sling and aimed it at Goliath. David let the sling out, and the stone flew high into the sky and hit the mighty giant right in the middle of his forehead.

Goliath's great body fell to the ground. David walked over to where the Philistine lay to make sure that he was really dead. Goliath did not move and David knew he had won the fight. When the Philistines saw that their hero had been beaten, they were very afraid. They abandoned their camps and ran away. The Israelites chased the Philistines a long way, fighting them with swords and spears. The Israelites had the power of God on their side and defeated the Philistines with ease. And all the people knew that there was a God in Israel, for David had shown that although he was small, he could defeat a huge giant with God's power to help him.

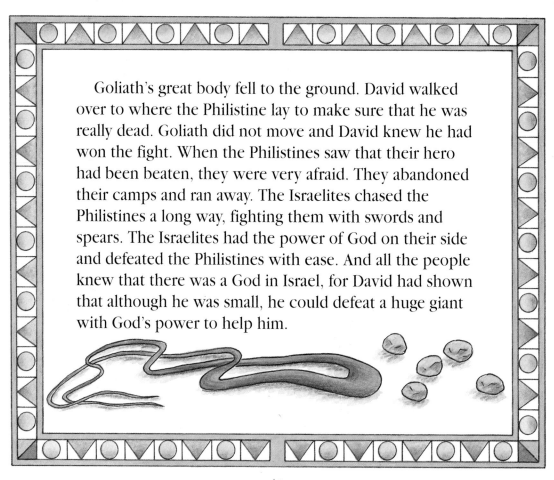

JONAH AND THE WHALE

Jonah was a good man, and God loved him. One day the Lord came to Jonah and said, "I want you to go to the great city of Nineveh. The people have become angry and are being cruel to each other, and you must tell them that I forbid them to continue their wickedness."

But Jonah was afraid of going to such a wicked place and instead of doing as God had commanded he ran away to escape. Jonah travelled to a nearby town called Joppa, where he found a boat just about to set sail. Jonah paid his fare and got onto the boat, thinking that he had

51

managed to trick God. But God knew Jonah was on the boat. He was
disappointed with Jonah and wanted to teach him a lesson,
so that he would not disobey him again. He waited
until the boat was far out at sea, then let loose
a huge wind and made the seas rise
high over the sides of the boat.
The sailors were afraid
for their lives.

The storm was the worst that they had ever seen and they knew that someone had made God angry. They threw the cargo over the side of the boat, to lighten the ship, and called out to their gods to help them. Meanwhile, Jonah had gone to his cabin below deck and had laid down to rest. The wind and rain did not bother him, and he had fallen fast asleep. The ship's captain was afraid for his crew and went to Jonah, who was the only person missing from the upper deck. He said, "How can you be asleep in this storm? You must get up and call on your God to save us."

All the sailors were very worried. They talked among themselves, trying to understand why such a bad storm had been sent to them. They turned on Jonah, who was a stranger, feeling sure he was to blame. "Where have you come from?" they asked him. "What are you doing on our boat?

Where are you going?" There were so many questions Jonah did not know which one to answer first.

"I am a Hebrew," he said, "I worship the Lord of all the seas and the land." When they heard this, the sailors were even more sure that Jonah was the cause of all their trouble, and asked, "What have you done wrong? We know that you are trying to escape." (When Jonah had come aboard he had told them he was trying to get away from something.)

The sailors asked Jonah what they could do to get rid of the storm. Jonah said, "You must throw me overboard. Then the sea will be calm again and the wind will die down. I know it is my fault that this terrible storm has come." The crew thought this was too cruel and tried to row back to shore. But the storm got worse and worse, the waves rose higher and the wind blew harder, so they had no choice but to do what Jonah had said. They took him and threw him overboard into the dark sea below. Immediately the sea grew calm and the rain stopped. The Lord sent a great whale to swallow Jonah and he slipped right down into its stomach. It was dark and cold inside, and there was a strong smell of seaweed. Jonah was very frightened and unhappy. For three days Jonah stayed in the stomach of the great whale, and each day he prayed to God for forgiveness.

God decided that Jonah had repented enough for disobeying him, and when the whale came close to land, it opened its huge mouth and let Jonah out onto the shore. Jonah was delighted to be back on dry land again.

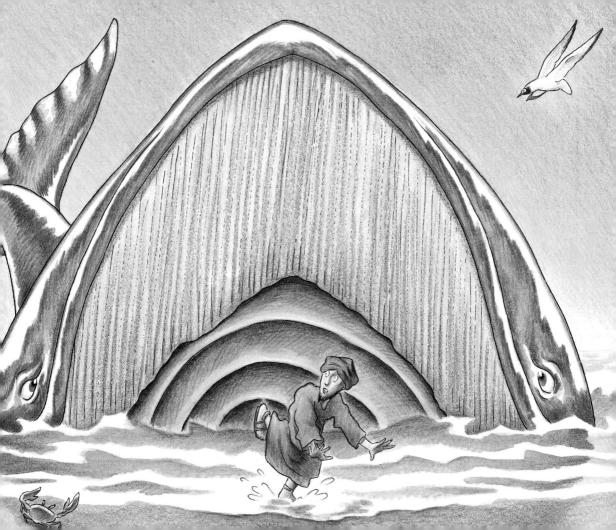

The Lord spoke to Jonah as he lay on the sand, commanding him to go straight to Nineveh and tell everyone that God was unhappy with their actions and that they must pray to him for forgiveness. Jonah did as he was told, and hurried off to the city. He had learned his lesson, and did not want to disobey God again.

It took Jonah a day to get to the city, and three days to travel through it, for it was a large city. When Jonah had come to a central place, a crowd gathered around him and he said to them, "In forty days the Lord will destroy your city." The people were afraid when they heard this, they knew that they had angered God. They declared a public fast and wore sackcloth to show that they were sorry for their bad behaviour. The rich and the poor alike prayed to the Lord. Even the King of Nineveh took off his rich clothes and jewellery and put on sackcloth.

The King made a public statement. He said, "We have all disobeyed God's laws. Everyone must leave behind their wicked ways and start a new life. We must all fast and wear sackcloth to try and please God."

The Lord saw that the people of Nineveh really had left their old habits behind and were truly sorry for their bad behaviour. He decided not to destroy them, but to let them live in peace.

But Jonah was angry with the Lord for not punishing the people as he had said he would. Jonah prayed to the Lord, saying, "Lord, I know that you are a good and gracious God, but you have let all these people go unpunished. I want you to take my life, because I would rather be dead than live in a place like this." The Lord answered Jonah gently, "Are you really so angry, that you want to die?"

God would not take Jonah's life. Jonah was miserable and left the city. He wandered out into the wilderness and sat with the hot sun beating down on him. The Lord saw this and felt sorry for Jonah sitting in the hot sun, so he made a shrub grow up beside Jonah to shade him. Jonah was grateful for the shrub, but the next day God sent a worm to attack the shrub and kill it. The shrub withered and died and left Jonah without any shade, sitting in the scorching sunshine. After a while he grew faint and prayed to God, again wishing that he was dead. The Lord said to Jonah, "Are you angry that the shrub died?"

"Yes," said Jonah. God replied, "But you did not plant it, nor look after it. The plant grew up and then died and you are sad that it died so soon. I would have been sad to destroy all the people of Nineveh. Therefore it is right to give them another chance and to let them live."